LET'S GO DOWN TO THE BEACH

Poems and Translations by William Lawlor

William Lawlor

LET'S GO DOWN TO THE BEACH

Poems and Translations by William Lawlor

◆

Featuring

Belkis Cuza Malé

Nicolás Guillén

Pedro Mir

Carlos Dobal

Poetry Harbor

A Poetry Harbor Publication

© 1996
Poetry Harbor
P.O. Box 103
Duluth, Minnesota 55801
Printed in Canada

ISBN: 0-9641986-9-X $13.95(US)
Cover art by Queen E. Brooks.

This book was made possible, in part, by a grant from the Arrowhead Regional Arts Council (with funding provided by the Minnesota State Legislature); and by Arts Midwest members and friends in partnership with the National Endowment for the Arts; and by Poetry Harbor members.

Some of these poems previously appeared in *South Coast Poetry Journal*, *Hepcat's Revenge*, *Pangloss Papers*, *The Gathering Post*, *Beatnik Soup*, *North Coast Review*, *Waterways*, *Ion*, *Broken Streets*, *Wisconsin Academy Review*, *Zest*, *Slant*, *Word of Mouth*, *Chequamegon Review*, *The Raddle Moon* and *Negative Capability*.

One photo of Nicolás Guillén appears courtesy of Keith Ellis, and it appeared in his book entitled *Cuba's Nicolás Guillén: Poetry and Ideology* published by the University of Toronto Press in 1983. A second photo appears courtesy of *Listín Diario*, and thanks go to Zaidy Zouain de Cruz for her help in acquiring the photo. A third photo of Guillén was taken by Osvaldo Salas and is provided courtesy of Agencia Literaria Latinoanmericana, and thanks go to Tania Jiménez for her help in acquiring the photo. The photo of Pedro Mir appears courtesy of *El Nuevo Diario*, and thanks go to Eusebia Peguero for her assistance in acquiring it. The photo of Carlos Dobal is by Fausto Foto and appears courtesy of Carlos Dobal. The photo of William Lawlor is by Joan McAuliffe. The photo of Belkis Cuza Malé is by William Lawlor.

Thanks to Belkis Cuza Malé for permission to publish and translate her poems. She retains the copyright to her poems. Thanks to Agencia Literaria Latinoanmericana for arranging permission to publish and translate the poems by Nicolás Guillén. Thanks to Pedro Mir for permission to publish and translate his poems. He retains the copyright to his poems. Thanks to Celeste Mir for help in acquiring permission. Thanks to Carlos Dobal for permission to publish and translate his poems. He retains the copyright to his poems.

Thanks to Queen E. Brooks, a 1994 Arts Midwest Fellowship recipient, for designing and hand-lettering the cover for this book, and for the use of her painting, "Ancestral Messenger," as part of the design.

Thanks to patrick mckinnon for his help in preparation of the manuscript for this book. Thanks to Linda Crawford and Eusebia Peguero for their assistance in proofreading the Spanish text. Thanks also to Peter Spooner.

For Valentina

and for my neighbors

LET'S GO DOWN TO THE BEACH
Poems and Translations by William Lawlor

Featuring Belkis Cuza Malé, Nicolás Guillén, Pedro Mir, and Carlos Dobal

◆

◆

ONE - *Poems*

¡AY, DIOS MIO!

I want this poem to repose

    like Cándido,

        my big Dominican friend,

who having finished

    nineteen beers,

        a dozen sausages,

            six fried corn cakes,

                a rack of ribs,

two large mangos,

    a plate of plantains,

        a pot of rice and beans,

            and four stiff drinks of rum,

moans as he drops

        into a soft, familiar chair.

THEY ARE AT FIRST AMAZED

I

in a new place and strange
they are at first amazed

their eyes brightening
the whole nation happy to hear

the accent fascination
the my name is what is your name

which way to the train
revelation of notfromhereness

eager to help
figuring out

dictionary thumbed
rules for exceptions

yes of course you sound so natural
where did you learn to speak

II

by gradations
Theirspeak speaking slow

listening
the months of repeat

would you please repeat
impatience rising

television heads
double speed depression

how long been here
you ought by now know

driving with bewildering friends
words of the song escape me

come on
why can't talk right

III

finally
almost a person

almost a voice
as if not

idiot
of idiom

invitation to dinner
confidence like wine

tie matching
language

tongue
expressive

words calm
as a napkin

IV

fatal then
in years that follow

crawling bug crushed
flight of insect squashed

the wriggling phrase
pinned in the air

the smiling of the first
who tells it to the second

who lets how can I forgive him
ha ha the whole nation know

what said was not
what ha ha thought said

worse worse
notfromhereness

LET'S GO DOWN TO THE BEACH

Let's go down to the beach
down the rocky twisting road to the beach
let's get in your tiny white car
and go down to the beach

where young men in shirts and shorts
await us with their cardboard panels
which they will put over your car
to keep it cool
and for a dollar they will watch your car
while we go down to the beach

Let's go down to Sosua Beach
where there is shade along the shore
shade in the sand and in clear sight of the sea
where eight brothers will crowd around us with eager faces
eight brothers from a father a hundred yards away
a father who grills fresh fish
a father with beer in a bucket of ice
let us go down to the beach
where one brother will bring us beer
and another brother will bring us fish in foil with tostones
let us go down to the beach
and eat this luscious lunch with our fingers
let us go down to the beach

Let's go down to the beach
where you will write a love note on a leaf
and I will write a love note on a leaf
and we will close our eyes and kiss
and when we open our eyes
a silent boy will be near us
a small silent boy
a boy so silent and so small that we will not have known his nearness
a boy who will mind his own business
who will wait to see if we want
more fish or beer
let's go down to the beach

Let's go down to the beach
to dream of what we will do when we are rich
to pretend that we own the villa on the hill
that rises from the sea

Let's go down to the beach
to hold hands
as the fisherman pushes his boat into the waves
as the clouds go on with their journey
to hold hands on Sosua Beach
let's go down to the beach

Let's go down to the beach and realize
we are in love
we have always been in love
we are in love

TWO - *Translations from Spanish*

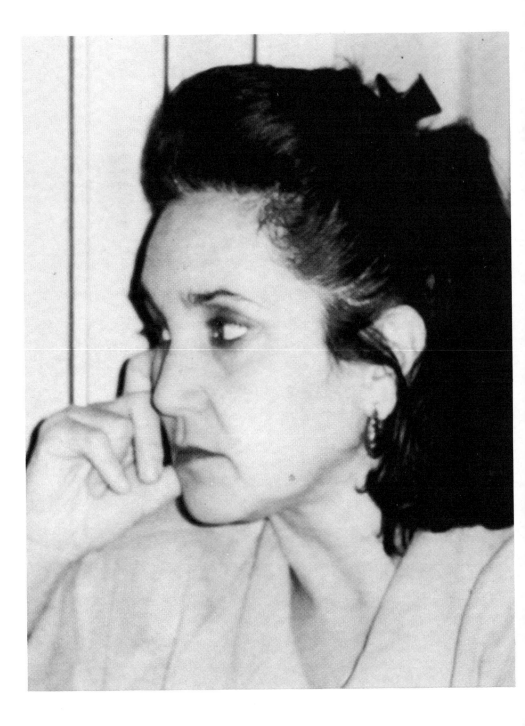

BELKIS CUZA MALÉ (1942-   )

Belkis Cuza Malé was born in Guantánamo, which lies in the easternmost part of the island of Cuba. After completing a master's degree in Hispanic-American and Cuban literature from Universidad del Oriente in 1964, she established herself in Havana as a journalist and poet, serving as a radio and television critic for the newspaper *Hoy*, working as editor of the cultural pages for the publication *Granma*, and writing and editing volumes of poetry, including *El viento en la pared, Ocho poetas*, and *Poesía cubana*. Of particular note are the collections *Tiempo de sol* and *Cartas a Ana Frank*, whose excellence was recognized by Casa de las Américas in 1963.

Eventually Belkis Cuza Malé (and her husband, the poet Heberto Padilla) came into conflict with the Castro administration and were arrested for "subversive writing." While their time spent in jail was not long, censorship and house arrest ensued. In particular, Malé's manuscript *Juego de damas*, which had reached the final stages of the Casa de las Américas competition in 1968, was shredded almost as soon as it came off the press.

"Who in today's world cares about a poem?" asks Malé. "Only and exclusively a customs official in a communist country. Only they believe in the efficacy of poetry. Although unwholesome as readers, they find it stimulating to think that one writes for someone: to play a dirty trick on a bureaucrat."

Malé has lived in the United States since 1979, both in Princeton, New Jersey, and in Miami, Florida. Her poetry has been included, in both Spanish and English, in various anthologies. A recurrent form in Malé's work is the biography of a writer filtered through the imagination of the biographer, and this method is revealed in *El clavel y la rosa* (1984), Malé's interpretation of the nineteenth-century Cuban poet Juana Borrero. In 1986, the Witter Bynner Foundation for Poetry assisted in the publication of *Woman on the Front Lines*, a bilingual anthology of selected poems. Her most recent work is *Elvis: la tumba sin sosiego o la verdadera historia de Jon Burrows*, published in both English and Spanish.

Malé recognizes her identity as a Cuban woman, but asserts her universality: "I also feel Spanish, Haitian, Mexican, and each one of the nationalities that pass by my side. My tragedy as a social being is minimized to the extent that I am the Jewess who managed to survive the atrocities of the concentration camp, the Hindu or Pakistani woman who contemplates with resignation the ceaseless waters of the sacred river in which her youth rots, the child who learned her ABC's in an African villàge, and I know I have lived the life of any Chinese girl. That's how I see myself, detached from the sun, fluttering like a butterfly, warbling among the leafy trees of Virginia."

Malé founded *Linden Lane Magazine* in 1982 and continues to edit and publish this literary tabloid featuring writing by Hispanic Americans, with an emphasis on Cubans in exile. For the *Nuevo Herald* in Miami, she writes a weekly column.

Although Malé and I corresponded occasionally for several years, the plans to publish this collection led to our first meeting, in Little Havana in 1995. As her poetry reveals, she is mystical, brooding, melancholy, and mysterious, but her faith and determination remain strong.

MANIQUI

La envidio,
ella usa un vestido dos piezas de Chanel,
una cartera de Gucci,
unos zapatos de Ferragamo.
La boca ríe con rojo de Estée Lauder
y Elizabeth Arden le delinea los ojos desafiantes.
De Ralph Lauren es el tatuaje de la piel,
y de Geoffrey Beene, las piernas.
Huele a Paloma Picasso, a agua de coco y a verbena,
no usa sostén,
pero el bikini es un diseño de Valentino.
Para el sol, cristales oscuros de la Loren.
Y a la hora de la verdad
nada como su Rolex con brillantes.
Ah, el alma le fue cortada y cosida en la casa Dior,
sobre hermosos brocados persas.

Si no me quisiera tanto a mí misma
me gustaría ser ella,
la dama fea del perrito.

April 19, 1991
from *Los poemas de la mujer de Lot*

MANNEQUIN

I envy her.
She wears a two-piece outfit by Chanel,
has a Gucci handbag,
Ferragamo shoes.
Her mouth laughs with Estée Lauder red
and Elizabeth Arden delineates her defiant eyes.
From Ralph Lauren comes the coloring of her skin,
and from Geoffrey Beene, that of her legs.
The fragrance of Paloma Picasso surrounds her—coconut milk and vervain.
She wears no bra,
but her bikini is a design by Valentino.
For the sun, dark glasses by Loren.
And at the hour of the truth
there's nothing like her Rolex with diamonds.
Ah, her soul was cut and sewn in the house of Dior
over beautiful Persian brocades.

If I didn't like myself so well
I would like to be her,
the ugly woman with the tiny dog.

CRITICA A LA RAZON IMPURA

Abre la puerta de su casa y entra
como un desconocido,
como si penetrara en el mundo
por la puerta de atrás.
En las paredes navega el barco
que grabó su hija,
la cuenta de la lavandaría
cuelga del palo mayor.
Sus vecinos han decidido casarse hoy
y pedirle por un rato los muebles.
Entra en su casa y comienza a escribir,
necesita arreglar el mundo de algún modo,
crear un hombre para ella,
una niñera para su hija
y un poco de vida para los gatos que no tiene.
Ella empieza a escribir,
como si estuviera delante de un jurado,
saca sus heroínas de papel,
porque ella es una muchacha que vive sola,
que duerme sola,
que baila sola.

Ella es la muchacha
que ustedes necesitan destruir
para sentirse más firmes.

from *Juego de damas* (1967)
inédito

CRITICISM OF IMPURE REASON

She opens the door of her house and goes in
like an unknown person,
as if she were penetrating the world
through the back door.
On the walls sails a ship
that her daughter drew,
the bill from the laundry
hangs from the mast.
Her neighbors have decided to marry today
and ask to use the furniture for a while.
She enters her house and begins to write,
she needs to adjust the world in some way,
create a man for herself,
a nanny for her daughter,
and a little bit of life for the cats she does not have.
She begins to write,
as if she were before a jury,
she takes her heroines from paper,
because she is a girl who lives alone
who sleeps alone,
who dances alone.

She is the girl
that you need to destroy
in order to feel strong.

PAJARO MIO

Junto a mí vuela un pájaro
que ha traído la noche y el agua,
un pájaro que viene aleteando y pidiendo
que cruza por encima de las cabezas y los sombreros,
un pájaro que parece gritarme AMOR ODIO,
un pájaro con su lanza y su pluma
su caballo dorado y su grueso abrigo de lentejuelas,
un pájaro amarillo, azul, verdecito,
una luna en cada mano, un diente de oro,
una pulsera y unos grilletes en los pies,
un pájaro senil, una diosa
dibujada en medio de la frente.
Un pájaro inventado por el cine,
un pájaro para tocarlo dulcemente como una melodía
de Stravinski,
un pájaro para comerlo en la hora de la angustia,
un pájaro para sentarlo entre las visitas,
un pájaro para dormirlo entre los brazos,
un pájaro para enterrarlo
con el cadáver enemigo,
un pájaro soñoliento que no me mira,
que quiere olfatearme,
besuquearme o lamerme como si yo fuera su caramelo,
como si en medio de tanto abrir los ojos,
no se hubiera rendido a las apariencias.

from *La otra mejilla*
inédito (1980-89)

MY BIRD

Together with me flies a bird
that has brought the night and the water,
a bird that comes fluttering and asking,
that crosses over heads and hats,
a bird that appears to shout at me LOVE HATE,
a bird with its thrust and feather,
its golden horse and thickly sequined coat,
a yellow bird, blue, distinctly green,
a moon in each hand, a golden tooth,
a bracelet and some shackles on its feet,
a senile bird, a goddess
with an ornamental design in the center of its chest.
A bird invented in the movies,
a bird to play it sweetly like a melody
from Stravinsky,
a bird good for eating in the hour of anguish,
a bird to sit down among the guests,
a bird to fall asleep in my arms,
a bird to bury
with the enemy corpse,
a drowsy bird that does not look at me,
that wants to smell me,
to lavish kisses on me or lick me as if I were its caramel candy,
as if in the act of opening the eyes so much
it had not given itself up to appearances.

CREDO

Si es verdad que hiciste la luz
y las sombras.
Si tu voz es inaudible
y tu mirada eterna
como tú mismo,
dime, por Dios, qué hago yo aquí,
tan pequeñita,
¿aguardando el cielo o el infierno?
Por favor, olvídate de mí
para bien y para mal.
Vivir en la cabeza de un pintor,
                   ser soñada.
Eso, sólo eso,
o una rama caída en el bosque.

from *La otra mejilla* (1975-1980)

BELKIS CUZA MALE

BELIEF

If it is true that you made the light
and the shadows.
If your voice cannot be heard
and your vision is eternal
like you yourself,
tell me, for God's sake, what I am doing here,
so tiny—
am I waiting for heaven or hell?
Please, forget about me
for good or for bad.
To live in the imagination of a painter,
                              to be dreamed.
That, only that,
or a fallen branch in the forest.

VIVIR SIN ESTAR ES SER

Hay un lugar, sin duda,
        donde vivo sin estar.
        Cuántos árboles y cuánta maleza
lo rodean,
pero yo lo alcanzo con sólo desearlo.
Allí, tras la ventana,
oyes los pájaros soñar despiertos,
que como tú también cantan para no morir.
Qué triste y qué solemne
esta mañana:
tu taza de té es un pozo en que te miras
sin reconocerme.
Y tus pasos resuenan invisibles sobre la loseta
de la cocina,
mientras yo te sigo a todas partes, gata o
quemadura de sol que se ha tatuado en tu cuerpo.

        ¿Quién eres si no el que escapó de sí mismo,
el que, como David, buscó refugio
en el pecho de Dios?
¿Y qué has hecho para merecer tanta pena,
o tanta soledad
o mi amor?

July 17, 1993
from *Los poemas de la mujer de Lot*

TO LIVE WITHOUT BEING SOMEWHERE IS TO BE

There is a place, no doubt,
        where I live without being there.
        How many trees and how many brambles
        surround it,
        but I reach it only by wishing.
        There, beyond the window,
        you hear the birds in their waking sleep
        that like you also sing so as not to die.
        How sad and solemn
        this morning:
        your cup of tea is a well in which you see yourself
        without recognizing me.
        And your steps resound invisible on the tiles
        of the kitchen,
        while I follow you everywhere, like a cat or
        sunburn that has colored your body.

        Who are you if not the one who has escaped from himself,
        he who, like David, sought refuge
        at the breast of God?
        And what have you done to deserve so much pain,
        or so much isolation
        or my love?

JUEGO DE DAMAS

No hay duda.
Alguien prepara su trampa,
está acechando con el ojo bueno,
mientras juega a la zurda como un tahur sin suerte.
Alguien se mueve impaciente en su sillón antiguo,
resopla un poco,
chasquea los dedos.
El amigo de la casa, el sabelotodo,
mira a un lado y otro convencido de que alguien
tiene que perder,
que la dama en rojo puede comerse a la dama en negro,
o viceversa.

No hay viento en la ventana, pero tampoco hay ventana,
sólo la noche.
No hay gatos en el techo, pero tampoco hay techo,
sólo el infierno
y un calorcito pegajoso.
Alguien hojea el diario, ¿pero qué importa
lo que sucede en China?
¿Qué importa que el Presidente Tal ya no presida nada?
¿Qué importan las estadísticas y los honorarios
de un caballero en ruina?
¿Qué importa el cadáver de Don Quijote?

El diario de la tarde trae su versión:
los dramas han pasado de moda.
Todo pasa, es cierto. Pero
¿a dónde va nuestro pasado?
¿Habrá un cielo o un infierno para él?

Uy,
la dama en negro avanza,
enseña sus pantorrillas por debajo de la mesa.
—¿Y ese ruido?, pregunta el marido.
Los niños de la casa,
los niños de la casa,
suenan sus tambores, tocan la sirena de alarma.
—Olvídalo, ha dicho la señora y continúa jugando.
—Son los niños. Sueñan.

El día de mañana . . .
¿Habrá mañana un día?
¿Y si hubiera otra cosa?

—No me cuentes más la historia del hombre y la mujer
que ya no se aman.
¿Cuánto hace que nos casamos?
Te amaré siempre,
y tú creerás que sigo siendo la mujer joven
y tímida que inventaste.

—No me mira. Oh espejo de paciencia,
oh soledad, oh torre de marfil,
oh cámara fotográfica.
¿Qué pensarán los hombres de los hombres?
No me mira. No me habla,
pero ¿quién ha visto una amante
cortejada fuera de la cama?

—No te he engañado nunca. Ni con el pensamiento.
Una mujer se casa para siempre,
hasta con el cadáver de ese hombre,
con sus manías y con su amante,
con su tos y con sus corbatas,
con su expediente de trabajo,
con las ciudades en que no fue nadie,
con la madre viuda y con el padre muerto,
con los hermanos y con sus esposas,
con su factor RH negativo,
con su semen, con el hígado y la posible neoplasia,
con los hijos que inventó cada noche,
con su máquina de afeitar
y la moral siniestra de todos los hombres.
Una mujer se casa para siempre.

—No te miro. No te hablo.
Tu voz me suena a Bach,
sube por mi boca,
toca mi sexo,
me desnuda.
Mañana voy a amarte como nunca.

¿De dónde viene este silencio?
¿Cuánto tiempo hace que ya no dices nada?
Te revuelves en tu sillón y fumas.
¿Y esas mujeres que se aferran a tu cuello?
¿Y esas damas que te devoran,
que gimen bajo tu aliento?
¿Y esos caballos que no son de angel,
y esas uñas,
y ese perfume,
y esas bocas,
y esas nalgas,
y esos culos,
y esa falsa inocencia con que te aman?

Saltas por la ventana,
huyes bajo el gran cielo de cartón.
El futuro no existe todavía
pero estás cogido en la trampa:

la dama en rojo se ha comido a la dama en negro,
o viceversa.

from *Juego de damas* (1967)
inédito

A GAME AMONG WOMEN

There is no doubt.
Someone prepares a trap,
she is spying with her good eye,
while she plays on the left like a card shark without luck.
Someone moves impatiently in his old easy chair,
snorts a little,
snaps his fingers.
The friend of the house, the know-it-all,
looks to one side and the other convinced that someone
must lose,
that the lady in red can eat the lady in black,
or the black the red.

There is no wind in the window, but neither is there a window,
only the night.
There are no cats on the roof, but neither is there a roof,
only hell
and a mild, sticky heat.
Someone glances through the newspaper, but what does it matter
what is happening in China?
What does it matter that President Such and Such now presides over nothing?
Who cares about the statistics and honoraria
of a gentleman in ruin?
What is the importance of the corpse of Don Quixote?

The afternoon paper brings its version:
The theater has gone out of style.
All things must pass, it is certain. But
where is our past going to?
Will there be a heaven or a hell for it?

Ay,
the woman in black comes forward,
she shows her calves under the table.
—And that noise? asks her husband.
The children of the house,
the children of the house,
they play their drums, they sound an alarm siren.
Forget it, the woman says and she continues playing.
They are the children. They dream.

The day of tomorrow . . .
Will there be tomorrow one day?
And might there be another thing?

You must not tell me more of the story of the man and the woman
that no longer love each other.
How long have we been married?
I will love you always,
and you will believe that I will continue being the young and timid woman
you invented.

He does not look at me. Oh mirror of patience
oh solitude, oh ivory tower,
oh camera.
What will the men think of the men?
He does not look at me. He does not talk to me,
but who has seen a lover
courted out of bed?

—I have never deceived you. Not even in thought.
A woman marries forever
until she is with the corpse of that man,
with his manias and with his lover,
with his cough and with his ties,
with his proficiency at work,
with the cities in which nobody went,
with the widowed mother and the dead father,
with the brothers and their wives,
with his RH negative factor,
with his semen, with the liver and the possible tumors,
with the children each night invented,
with his electric shaver
and the sinister morality of all men.
A woman marries forever.

I don't look at you. I don't talk to you.
Your voice sounds like Bach,
it rises in my mouth,
it makes me feel sexy,
it strips me naked.
Tomorrow I am going to love you as never before.

Where does this silence come from?
How long has it been that you say nothing?
You turn in your seat and you smoke.
And these women who cling to your collar?
And these women who devour you,
who howl under your breath?
And that hair that is not of an angel,
and those fingernails,
and that perfume,
and those mouths,
and those buttocks,
and those asses,
and that phony innocence with which they love you?

You jump from the window,
you run under the great cardboard sky.
The future still doesn't exist
but you are caught in the trap:

The woman in red has eaten the woman in black,
or the black the red.

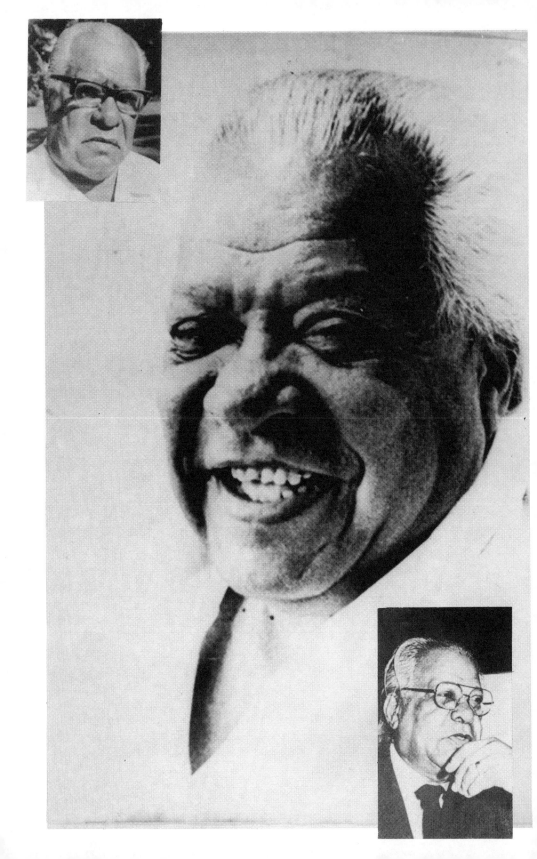

NICOLAS GUILLEN (1902-1989)

Nicolás Guillén was born in Camaguey, the third largest city in Cuba. In that city he began his schooling, and from his father, a journalist who was politically active, Guillén also learned the skills of typography and printing. He began undergraduate studies at the University of Havana, but did not complete a degree.

Extraordinarily prolific, Guillén is an influential author. During his life, his journeys took him to dozens of nations around the world, where he read his work and participated in innumerable conferences. His poetry, which masterfully blends rhythms, humor, rhyme, and political statements, has the power to both charm and provoke, and the appeal of his poetry has led to dozens of major awards and translations into at least twenty-six languages. He is known as the National Poet of Cuba.

In the United States, his work is especially significant to those connected with the struggle of blacks, as is evidenced by the collection of translations entitled *Cuba Libre* (1948) prepared by Langston Hughes and Ben F. Carruthers and the translation of *Tengo* (1974) by Richard J. Carr published by Broadside Press. In "Little Rock" Guillén fiercely criticizes racial intolerance in the United States, and in "Tengo" the poem's speaker takes satisfaction in the improvement in Cuban civil rights accomplished by the Cuban Revolution. Today Guillén is frequently referred to with admiration and respect by activists like Amiri Baraka and Sonia Sanchez.

To list the titles of Guillén's numerous volumes of poetry is beyond the scope of these pages. In Cuba at least thirty-four titles bear his name, including *Motivos de son* (1930), *West Indies, Ltd.* (1934), *La paloma de vuelo popular* (1958), *Tengo* (1964), and *El gran zoo* (1967). Numerous editions are available across Latin America. An excellent collection which includes most of his poetry is *Obra Poética* (Editorial Letras Cubanas, 1985), and this two-volume work features a helpful bibliography and biographical chronology.

In the poems I translate here, I seek to capture Guillén's celebration of the common man. In "A la Virgen de la Caridad," the author playfully reveals the confounding frustration the church offers to the poor. In "Soneto: a un amigo, proponiéndole la reconciliación," Guillén shows how the delight of ordinary food can help friends set aside their differences. Both "Tengo" and "Little Rock" strike out at social injustice, but the central focus is once again on ordinary people.

SONETO

A un amigo,
proponiéndole la reconciliación

Como sé que te gusta almorzar fuerte
y un almuerzo español es bien forzudo,
vengo (con un soneto por escudo)
a dar fin almorzando a un duelo a muerte.

¿El tocino te encanta o te divierte?
¿Prefieres el jamón servido crudo?
Platos hay que farán fablar a un mudo.
Frente a ellos, por Dios, quisiera verte.

Pelillos a la mar y sin tardanza
corramos presto a la sagrada fonda
donde hierve el puchero y se agarbanza:

La cazuela está allí, ventruda y honda . . .
Cante otra vez sus himnos la esperanza
y a la amistad el corazón responda.

(1964)
from *Obra Poética*

SONNET

to a friend, proposing reconciliation

Because I know that you like a big lunch
and a Spanish lunch is very heavy
I come (with a sonnet as a shield)
to put to an end by eating lunch a duel unto the death.

The bacon, does it charm you or give you pleasure?
Would you prefer to be served a ham that is cured?
There exist dishes that will bring words to the mouth of a mute.
With such plates in front of you, my God, I would like to see you.

Let's bury the hatchet, and without delay
we should run at once to the sacred inn
where the stew simmers and becomes a beany soup.

The stew pot is there, oval-shaped and deep . . .
Hope must sing again its hymns
and to friendship the heart will respond.

TENGO

Cuando me veo y toco
yo, Juan sin Nada no más ayer,
y hoy Juan con Todo,
y hoy con todo,
vuelvo los ojos, miro,
me veo y toco
y me pregunto cómo ha podido ser.

Tengo, vamos a ver,
tengo el gusto de andar por mi país,
dueño de cuanto hay en él,
mirando bien de cerca lo que antes
no tuve ni podía tener.
Zafra puedo decir,
monte puedo decir,
ciudad puedo decir,
ejército decir,
ya míos para siempre y tuyos, nuestros,
y un ancho resplandor
de rayo, estrella, flor.

Tengo, vamos a ver,
tengo el gusto de ir
yo, campesino, obrero, gente simple,
tengo el gusto de ir
(es un ejemplo)
a un banco y hablar con el administrador,
no en inglés,
no en señor,
sino decirle compañero como se dice en español.

Tengo, vamos a ver,
que siendo un negro
nadie me puede detener
a la puerta de un dancing o de un bar.
O bien en la carpeta de un hotel
gritarme que no hay pieza,
una mínima pieza y no una pieza colosal,
una pequeña pieza donde yo pueda descansar.

Tengo, vamos a ver,
que no hay guardia rural
que me agarre y me encierre en un cuartel,
ni me arranque y me arroje de mi tierra
al medio del camino real.
Tengo que como tengo la tierra tengo al mar,
no country,
no jailáif,
no tenis y no yacht,
sino de playa en playa y ola en ola,
gigante azul abierto democrático:
en fin, el mar.

Tengo, vamos a ver,
que ya aprendí a leer,
a contar,
tengo que ya aprendí a escribir
y a pensar
y a reír.
Tengo que ya tengo
donde trabajar
y ganar
lo que tengo que comer.
Tengo, vamos a ver,
tengo lo que tenía que tener.

(1964)
from *Obra Poética*

I HAVE

When I see and pinch myself,
I, Juan Who Has Nothing, yesterday nothing more,
and today Juan Who Has All,
and today with everything,
I turn my eyes, I look,
I see and pinch myself
and I ask myself how this has come to be.

I have, we are going to see,
I have the pleasure of walking in my country,
owner of that which is in it,
seeing well and near to me that which before
I neither had nor was able to have.
The sugar harvest I can say,
the hillsides I can say,
the city I can say,
the army I can say,
now mine forever and yours, ours,
and a wide brilliance
of ray, star, flower.

I have, we will see,
I have the pleasure of going
I, campesino, worker, simple person,
I have the pleasure of going
(it is an example)
to a bank to talk with the administrator,
not in English
not saying "sir"
but to say to him, as one says in Spanish, "compañero."

I have, we are going to see,
I, being a black person,
have the certainty that nobody can detain me
at the door of a disco or of a bar.
Nor in the lobby of a hotel
shout at me that there is no room,
no minimal room, no colossal room,
no tiny room where I might rest.

I have, we shall see,
I have the satisfaction
that there are no troops in the countryside
who grab me and shut me in a cell,
no troops who bump me and drive me from my land
into the middle of the roadway.
I have the land as I have the sea,
no house in the country,
no high life,
no tennis and no yacht,
but from beach to beach and wave to wave,
giant, open, democratic blue,
at last, the sea.

I have, we will see,
I have the contentment
that I have learned to read,
to tell stories,
I have learned to write
and to think
and to laugh.
I have a place
to work
and earn
that which I have to eat.
I have, we are going to see,
I have that which I had to have.

A LA VIRGEN DE LA CARIDAD

Virgen de la Caridad,
que desde un peñón de cobre
esperanza das al pobre
y al rico seguridad.
En tu criolla bondad,
¡oh madre!, siempre creí,
por eso pido de ti
que si esa bondad me alcanza
des al rico la esperanza,
la seguridad a mí.

(1964)
from *Obra Poética*

♦ *NICOLAS GUILLEN*

TO THE VIRGIN OF CHARITY

Virgin of Charity,
who from the Rock of Copper Ore
gives hope to the poor
and to the rich security,
in thy native generosity,
oh Mother! I always have believed
and because of that I ask to receive.
If to me generosity reaches out
give to the rich a world to hope about
and give security to me.

LITTLE ROCK

a Enrique Amorim

Un blues llora con lágrimas de música
en la mañana fina.
El Sur blanco sacude
su látigo y golpea. Van los niños
negros entre fusiles pedagógicos
a su escuela de miedo.
Cuando a sus aulas lleguen,
Jim Crow será el maestro,
hijos de Lynch serán sus condiscípulos
y habrá en cada pupitre
de cada niño negro,
tinta de sangre, lápices de fuego.

Así es el Sur. Su látigo no cesa.

En aquel mundo faubus,
bajo aquel duro cielo faubus de gangrena,
los niños negros pueden
no ir junto a los blancos a la escuela.
O bien quedarse suavemente en casa.
O bien (nunca se sabe)
dejarse golpear hasta el martirio.
O bien no aventurarse por las calles.
O bien morir a bala y a saliva.
O no silbar al paso de una muchacha blanca.
O en fin, bajar los ojos yes,
doblar el cuerpo yes,
arrodillarse yes,
en aquel mundo libre yes
de que habla Foster Tonto en aeropuerto y aeropuerto,
mientras la pelotilla blanca,
una graciosa pelotilla blanca,
presidencial, de golf, como un planeta mínimo,
rueda en el césped puro, terso, fino,
verde, casto, tierno, suave, yes.

Y bien, ahora,
señoras y señores, señoritas,

ahora niños,
ahora viejos peludos y pelados,
ahora indios, mulatos, negros, zambos,
ahora pensad lo que sería
el mundo todo Sur,
el mundo todo sangre y todo látigo,
el mundo todo escuela de blancos para blancos,
el mundo todo Rock y todo Little,
el mundo todo yanqui, todo faubus . . .
                    Pensad por un momento,
imaginadlo un solo instante.

(1958)
from *Obra Poética*

♦ *NICOLAS GUILLEN*

LITTLE ROCK

for Enrique Amorim

A blues tune cries musical tears
in the fine morning.
The white South unleashes
its whip and strikes. The Negro children
pass between the pedagogical rifles
to their school of fear.
When they arrive at their classes
Jim Crow will be their teacher,
the sons of Lynch will be their classmates
and there will be at each lecture seat
of each Negro child
ink of blood, pens of fire.

That's the way the South is. Its whip is relentless.

In that world of Governor Faubus
under that hard, gangrenous sky of Governor Faubus
the black children can
not go together with the whites to school.
Or else stay softly at home.
Or else (one never knows)
yield themselves to be beaten into martyrdom.
Or else not venture into the streets.
Or else die by bullet or spit.
Or not whistle at the walk of a white girl.
Or finally, lower the eyes yes,
bend the body yes,
kneel down yes,
in that free world yes
of which Foster Fool speaks from airport to airport,
while the little white ball,
a gracious little white ball,
presidential, of golf, like a minimal planet,
rolls in the pure turf, short, fine,
green, chaste, tender, soft, yes.

And even now,
ladies and gentlemen,

now children,
now old folks shaggy haired and freshly barbered,
now Indians, mulattoes, blacks, mestizos,
now think whatever might be
a whole world like this South,
the world all blood and all whip,
the world all white schools for whites,
the world all Rock and all Little,
the world all Yankee, all Governor Faubus . . .
                    Think for a moment,
Imagine it a single instant.

PEDRO MIR (1913-   )

When asked where the inspiration for poetry comes from, Pedro Mir, the National Poet of the Dominican Republic, answers, "From suffering." Yet Mir is quick to add that there is nothing at all romantic or glamorous about this suffering.

In Mir's life, suffering came in the form of an exile from the Dominican Republic which began in 1947. The powerful dictatorship of Trujillo stood ominously in the path of the poet, and Mir left for Cuba. He did not return until 1962, when Trujillo was already in the grave.

In the case of Mir's country, whose history Mir has recorded, analyzed, and interpreted in numerous scholarly works, the suffering has come down through centuries. Mir compares the Dominican Republic to "an adolescent girl kicked in the hips." Mir's poetry and other writings draw power from Mir's artistic combination of his personal struggle and the struggle of his nation.

Following Mir's return to Santo Domingo in 1962, the verse he produced while in exile, which includes "Hay un país en el mundo," "Si alguién me pregunta cuál es mi país" and "Contracanto a Walt Whitman (canto a nostotros mismos)," won the hearts and minds of the Dominican people, who turned out in the thousands for readings. In 1982, the Dominican legislature named Mir the National Poet of the Dominican Republic. In 1991, Hunter College of the City University of New York awarded Mir an honorary doctorate, and in 1993, Mir received the National Prize for Literature in the Dominican Republic.

Though Pedro Mir is consistently serious in his poetry, his conversation reveals a sharply witty style. When he met me at his home in Santo Domingo, he momentarily thought about my arrival with my wife, Valentina Peguero, a well-known Dominican historian. She had arranged the meeting.

"You know," he said, maintaining a serious stare, "you could have come by yourself. You didn't have to come with Valentina."

Then, after pausing a second, he added, teasing me just a bit, "But maybe it is better that you came with her."

Mir's frankness and his readiness to challenge ideas are the keys to his wit. When I suggested that there is a contradiction in poets who oppose materialism in their poetry and then sell tickets to their appearances at high prices, Mir became animated: "You *must* pay. When Arthur Rubinstein gives a concert, you must pay to hear the music, and so it is with the poet, for like any other worker, a poet must support his family. I was at a gathering once, and after I read my poems, the woman reached for the flower arrangement on the table and presented the bouquet to me. I thought, 'Lady, the flowers are very beautiful, but where is the check?'"

Pedro Mir emphasizes the importance and influence of Walt Whitman on Latin American literary culture. He doubts that people in the United States appreciate and admire Walt Whitman as much as Latin Americans do. The importance of Whitman to Mir is evident in the freedom taken in the length and placement of the lines as well as the accumulation of specific details in catalogs, but most clear in the emphasis on how a poet and a nation combine to know themselves—their beauty and their pain. Mir's poetry brings to life the rivers and the mountains of Hispaniola, as well as the bays, sugar fields, and forests, revealing Pedro Mir's intimacy with his homeland.

An excellent bilingual edition of Mir's work is *Countersong to Walt Whitman and Other Poems* (Azul Editions, 1993), a translation by Jonathan Cohen and Donald D. Walsh. Silvio Torres Saillant of the Dominican Studies Institute at the City University of New York provides a valuable introduction.

de HAY UN PAIS EN EL MUNDO
poema gris en varias ocasiones

¡Ah, desventurados!—exclamó indignado el sirio—¿Cómo imaginar semejante exceso de rabia furiosa? Me dan ganas de dar tres pasos y aplastar de tres patadas a todo ese hormiguero de ridículos asesinos . . .

No os toméis ese trabajo—le respondieron—. Ellos mismos se encargan de su ruina.

Voltaire, *Micromegas,* cap. VII

Hay
un país en el mundo
                    colocado
en el mismo trayecto del sol.
Oriundo de la noche.
                    Colocado
en un inverosímil archipiélago
de azúcar y de alcohol.
                         Sencillamente
liviano,
         como un ala de murciélago
apoyado en la brisa.
                     Sencillamente
claro,
       como el rastro del beso en las solteras
antiguas
         o el día en los tejados.
                                  Sencillamente
frutal. Fluvial. Y material. Y sin embargo
sencillamente tórrido y pateado
como una adolescente en las caderas.
Sencillamente triste y oprimido.
Sinceramente agreste y despoblado.

En verdad.
Con tres millones
                 suma de la vida
y entre tanto
              cuatro cordilleras cardinales
y una inmensa bahía y otra inmensa bahía,

tres penínsulas con islas adyacentes
y un asombro de ríos verticales
y tierra bajo los árboles y tierra
bajo los ríos y en la falda del monte
y al pie de la colina y detrás del horizonte
y tierra desde el canto de los gallos
y tierra bajo el galope de los caballos
y tierra sobre el día, bajo el mapa, alrededor
y debajo de todas las huellas y en medio del amor.
Entonces
      es lo que he declarado.
                 Hay
un país en el mundo
sencillamente agreste y despoblado.

(1949)

from THERE IS A COUNTRY IN THE WORLD
a gray poem for several occasions

"Oh, the misguided!" exclaimed the indignant Syrian. "How could one imagine this outpouring of furious anger? It is to my advantage to take three steps and squash in three kicks all of this anthill of ridiculous assassins . . . "

"You do not have to undertake all that work," they responded. "They themselves are in charge of their ruin."

Voltaire, *Micromegas*, VII

There is
a country in the world
                    placed
in the path of the sun.
Born of the night.
                    Placed
in an unbelievable group of islands
of sugar and alcohol.
                    Simply
light,
        like the wing of a bat
supported by a breeze.
                    Simply
clear,
        like the impression of kisses on unmarried Victorian
women
            or like a day spent on the rooftops.
                            Simply
like a garden of fruits. Fluvial. And material. And nevertheless
simply torrid and kicked
like an adolescent in her hips.
Simply sad and oppressed.
Honestly rustic and unpopulated.

In truth.
With the sum
                    of three million lives
and at the same time
                        there are four vertical mountain ranges

and a giant bay and another giant bay,
three peninsulas with adjacent islands
and an amazing number of vertical rivers
and land beneath the trees and land
under the rivers and at the edge of the forest
and at the foot of the mountain and beyond the horizon
and land from the crow of the cocks
and land under the hooves of the horses
and land throughout the day, under the map, around
and under all the footprints and in the middle of love.
Therefore
            it is that which I have said.
                                    There is
a country in the world
simply rustic and unpopulated.

de CONCIERTO DE ESPERANZA PARA LA MANO IZQUIERDA

SOLO DE ESPERANZA

La esperanza es un nido
y una semilla en el suelo.
La esperanza es una flor
en forma de coliflor
que mastican lejanos
los camellos.
La esperanza es la raíz
en la humedad, y el arroyo
en el desierto.
El barco sobre la mar
y Federico en sus versos.
La esperanza es un concierto
popular
en los años duros
y en doscientos muertos.
El caballo en la montaña
y en Granada un monumento.
La esperanza es un cuartel
de policía consagrado
a cuidar la tranquilidad
del pensamiento
el orden del arcoíris
y la equidad del recuerdo.
La esperanza es la esperanza
convertida en ley
de los pueblos,
el pueblo convertido en ley
y la esperanza en Gobierno.
La esperanza es un Estado
de muchachas escribiendo
un plan quinquenal de niños
y una constitución del soneto.
La esperanza es contar con todo
lo que necesita el librero
y el obrero de obras públicas
para trazar un camino

que una a todos los pueblos
del mundo,
convierta a todas las patrias
en una sola patria,
reúna todos los brazos
en un solo trabajo
sideral y alegre,
lleve la flor y la coliflor
a los desiertos,
traiga invasiones de trigo
y de manzana a los centrales
azucareros.
Un río de lunas que gira
en el corazón del sistema
planetario y derrama
la médula del hombre
sobre la espuma del
firmamento.
La esperanza es la muerte
de lo que fuera antiguo
y ha sido eterno.
La esperanza es la muerte de la muerte.
La esperanza es la esperanza
de reanudar la juventud del pueblo.

(1969)

from CONCERTO OF HOPE FOR THE LEFT HAND

SOLO OF HOPE

Hope is a nest
and a seed in the soil.
Hope is a flower
in the form of a cauliflower
that far-off
camels chew.
Hope is the root
in the dampness, and the brook
in the desert.
The ship at sea
and Federico in his poetry.
Hope is a concerto
popular
in the years of difficulty
and in two hundred deaths.
The horse in the mountains
and in Grenada a monument.
Hope is a police precinct
devoted
to watch over the tranquility
of thought
the order of the rainbow
the equity of remembrance.
Hope is hope
made into the law
of the people,
the people converted into law
and hope into Government.
Hope is a State
of girls writing
a five-year plan for children
and a constitution from the sonnet.
Hope is to rely on all things
that which the bookseller needs
and the worker on public projects
to plot a path
that joins all people
of the world,

converts all countries
to a single country,
joins all arms
in a single work
configured like a constellation and happy,
takes the flower and the cauliflower
to the deserts,
brings invasions of wheat
and apples to the sugar mills.
A river of moons that gyrates
in the heart of the planetary
system and spills
the substance of man
over the effervescence of the
firmament.
Hope is the death
of that which was ancient
and has been eternal.
Hope is the death of death.
Hope is hope
to renew the youth of the people.

de SI ALGUIEN QUIERE SABER CUAL ES MI PATRIA

Si alguien quiere saber cuál es mi patria
no la busque,
no pregunte por ella.

Siga el rastro goteante por el mapa
y su efigie de patas imperfectas.
No pregunte si viene del rocío
o si tiene espirales en las piedras
o si tiene sabor ultramarino
o si el clima le huele en primavera.
No la busque ni alargue las pupilas.
No pregunte por ella.

(¡Tanto arrojo en la lucha irremediable
y aún no hay quien lo sepa!
¡Tanto acero y fulgor de resistir
y aún no hay quien lo vea!)

No, no la busque.
Si alguien quiere saber cuál es mi patria,
no pregunte por ella.
No quiera saber si hay bosques, trinos,
penínsulas muchísimas y ajenas,
o si hay cuatro cadenas de montañas,
todas derechas,
o si hay varios destinos de bahías
y todas extranjeras.

Siga el rastro goteando por la brisa
y allí donde la sombra se presenta,
donde el tiempo castiga y desmorona,
ya no la busque,
no pregunte por ella.
Su propia sangre, su órbita querida,
su instantáneo chispazo de presencia,
su funeral de risa y de sonrisa,
su potrero de espaldas indirectas,
su puño de silencio en cada boca,
su borbotón de ira en cada mueca,
sus manos enguantadas en la fábrica y

sus pies descalzos en la carretera,
las largas cicatrices que le bajan
como antiguos riachuelos, su siniestra
figura de mujer
obligada a parir
con cada coz que busca su cadera
para echar una fila de habitantes
listos para la rueda,
todo dirá de pronto dónde existe
una patria moderna.
Dónde habrá que buscar y qué pregunta
se solicita. Porque apenas
surge la realidad y se apresura
una pregunta, ya está la respuesta.

No, no la busque.
Tendría que pelear por ella . . .

(1949)

from IF SOMEONE WANTS TO KNOW
WHICH COUNTRY IS MINE

If someone wants to know which country is mine,
don't look for her,
don't ask for her.

Follow the footprints dripping from the map
and her effigy of imperfect feet.
Don't ask if she is coming from the dew
or if she has spires in her stones
or if she has a taste of the deep blue sea
or if the climate is fragrant in the spring.
Don't look for her or open wide your eyes.
Don't ask for her.

(So much boldness in the unsolvable struggle
and though there is nobody who might know it!
So much steel and effulgence in resistance
and though there is nobody who sees it!)

No, don't look for her.
If someone wants to know which country is mine,
don't ask for her.
You would not want to know if there are forests, the warbling of birds,
many and distant peninsulas,
or if there are four chains of mountains,
all straight,
or if there are ports in bays
and all foreign.

Follow the footsteps dripping in the breeze
and there where the shadow appears,
where time punishes and pulverizes,
no longer look for her,
don't ask for her.
Her own blood, her beloved sphere,
the instantaneous flaring of her being into presence,
her funeral of laughter and smiles,
her pastures that turn their backs,
her fist of silence in every mouth,

her boiling ire in every grimace,
her hands gloved in the factory and
her bare feet in the roadway,
the long scars that streak her
like ancient streams, her sinister
female figure
obliged to give birth
with each kick aimed at her hips
to generate a line of inhabitants
ready for the torture table,
all will say at once where there is
a modern country.
Where one has to look and what question
one has to ask. Because at the moment that
reality arises and a question
forces itself, already there is an answer.

No, don't look for her.
You would have to fight for her . . .

de CONTRACANTO A WALT WHITMAN
(Canto a nosotros mismos)

13.

Si queréis encontrar el duro acento moderno
de la palabra
                    yo
                        id a Santo Domingo.
Pasad por Nicaragua. Preguntad en Honduras.
Escuchad al Perú, a Bolivia, a la Argentina.
Dondequiera hallaréis un capitán sonoro
                                        un yo.
Un jefe luminoso,
                un yo, un cosmos,
Un hombre providencial,
                un yo, un cosmos, un hijo de su patria.
Y en el medio de la noche fragorosa de la América
escucharéis, detrás de madureces y fragancias,
mezclados con sordos quejidos, con blasfemias y gritos,
con sollozos y puños, con largas lágrimas y largas
aristas y maldiciones largas
                un yo, Walt Whitman, un cosmos,
                un hijo de Manhattan.
Una canción antigua convertida en razón de fuerza
entre los engranajes de las factorías, en las calles
de las ciudades. Un yo, un cosmos, en las guardarrayas,
y en los vagones y en los molinos de los centrales.
Una canción antigua convertida en razón de sangre y de miseria,
un yo, un Walt Whitman, un cosmos,
¡un hijo de Manhattan . . . !

(1952)

from SONG IN ANSWER TO WALT WHITMAN (song to ourselves)

13.

If you want to hear the hard modern accent
of the word
   I
    go to Santo Domingo.
Go to Nicaragua. Ask in Honduras.
Listen in Peru, Bolivia, Argentina.
Wherever you go you will encounter a sonorous Captain
    an I.
A shining chief,
    an I, a cosmos,
A providential man,
    an I, a cosmos, a son of his nation.
And in the middle of the thunderous American night
you will hear, beyond ripenesses and fragrances,
blended with muffled moans, with blasphemies and shouts,
with sobs and fists, with long tears and long
edges and long curses
    an I, Walt Whitman, a cosmos,
    of Manhattan the son.
An ancient song transformed into force
in the grinding gears of the factories,
   in the streets
of the cities. An I, a cosmos, in the territorial boundaries
and in the railway cars and in the sugar mills.
An ancient song transformed into blood
   and misery,
an I, a Walt Whitman, a cosmos,
of Manhattan the son!

CARLOS DOBAL (1926-   )

Carlos Dobal is Emeritus Professor of History at Pontificia Universidad Católica Madre y Maestra in Santiago, the Dominican Republic. Born in Havana, Cuba, of a Dominican father and a Cuban mother, he completed his doctoral studies at the University of Havana. He is distinguished for his term of service as Ambassador to the Vatican from the Dominican Republic, his numerous scholarly investigations of history, and his membership in the Dominican Academy of History.

The discovery that this historian and diplomat is also a poet came as a surprise to me when we had occasion to meet and converse regularly in the Dominican Republic in 1983. Dobal's volumes of poetry, which stand among numerous historical studies, include *Poemas* (1975), *Variaciones* (1977) and *Otros* (1982), and in these volumes, Dobal reveals his uncanny ability to compare and combine sensory experiences and to build harmonies based on apparent antitheses.

In my translations of Dobal's poetry, I try to capture what distinguished Dominican poet Hector Inchaustegui Cabral calls the "apparent innocence" and "apparent simplicity" in Dobal's poetry. The lines are short, the rhythm is often fast paced, and the theme seems immediately accessible. However, the poems embody a subtle complexity, for as Cabral remarks, "The fruit interests [Dobal] more than the flower, action interests him more than the promise of action, existence interests him more than programs."

In "El crimen," Dobal's materials—a crack in the wall, an ant, and a single finger—raise issues of morality and mortality. In "Astronauta," the materials are the elements of man in space, yet the real issue is the nature of the senses. "Oyendo *Rhapsody in Blue*" returns to sensory experience, but also gives access to the nature of memory and music. Finally, "Poema de las doce" transforms the simple page into the object of artistic fulfillment.

Of the poems presented on these pages, "Canción por mis veinte amores desesperados" stands as Dobal's finest achievement. On one hand, the poem reveals Dobal's meticulous education and refinement as the lines include references to Malaparte, Maillol, Cellini and Goya, yet on the other hand the poem is more than a professorial display of knowledge. In "Canción," Dobal is personal and introspective, retracing his youth with witty honesty and clever reflection.

On a warm evening in Santiago, Dobal gave my wife and me a personal reading as we sat in chairs in his living room. On that night, we were charmed by the poem and honored to be his private audience. When the occasion arose to publish this collection of translations, I immediately recalled Dobal's special poem, and I thank Dobal for his confidence in me as his friend and translator.

ASTRONAUTA

Hubo una vez,
quien quiso
atar el silencio
a su pupila
y subió
a la estratósfera
en carro tirado,
por mil truenos
químicos.

Rota la barrera
del sonido
escarlata,
el silencio,
incoloro,
comenzó
a inundar sus arterias
de un elixir
insípido . . .

El potente silencio
ganó y venció
al umbral
sensible
de su diástole . . .
y pronto,
su ojo
—sorprendido—
comenzó a percibir
cómo el dolor
volvía a tomar
el mismo
color escarlata
del sonido.

from *Otros* (1983)

♦ *CARLOS DOBAL*

ASTRONAUT

Once upon a time,
someone wanted
to fasten silence
to the center of his eye
and he soared
into the stratosphere
in a car propelled
by a thousand
chemical thunders.

With the scarlet
sound barrier broken,
with the silence
colorless,
his arteries
began to flood
with a tasteless
elixir . . .

The strong silence
reached and surpassed
the threshold
of feeling
of his expanded heart . . .
and quickly
his eye
—surprised—
began to perceive
how the pain
was beginning to take
the same
scarlet color
as the sound.

♦ *CARLOS DOBAL*

EL CRIMEN

Hay una sorpresa
en esta grieta
de la pared
que parece copiar
en su curso
la ruta
del Nilo . . .
Es una vida
mínima:
una hormiga.

Allí, acomodados
a la herida
—de canto y cal—
están
sus dos antenas
torcidas;
la tenaza brutal
de su boca
y el resorte sutil
de su inquina.

Pero este
ínfimo corpúsculo
está animado
por la vida . . .
y cuando mi dedo
insensible,
destruye su sentido,
comete,
indiferente,
un crimen . . .

from *Otros* (1983)

THE CRIME

There is a surprise
in this crack
in the wall
that appears to follow
the path
of the Nile . . .
It is a minimal life:
an ant.

There, comfortable
in the wound
in the masonry
are two
crooked antennae;

The brute pincers
of its mouth
and the delicate spring
of its aversion.

But this
tiny corpuscle
is charged with life . . .
and when my
insensitive finger
destroys the meaning of such life,
I commit,
without thinking,
a crime . . .

♦ *CARLOS DOBAL*

OYENDO "RHAPSODY IN BLUE"

Recordar es abrir
un camino azul
entre presente y pasado:
marino y aéreo azul
entre dos tonalidades
de un mismo color,
en dos intensidades
de un solo calor,
en dos rayos de único
fulgor . . .
Recordar es cerrar un camino azul
entre placer y dolor.

from *Poemas* (1975)

♦ *CARLOS DOBAL*

ON HEARING "RHAPSODY IN BLUE"

To remember is to open
a blue path
between present and past:
the blue of the sea and the sky
between two tonalities
of a singular color,
in two intensities
of a singular heat,
in two rays from a singular
splendor . . .
To remember is to close a blue path
between pleasure and pain.

POEMA DE LAS DOCE

La página virgen se ofrece desnuda
en piel y lágrimas,
sobre mi escritorio,
en la noche clara.

Su tierna nitidez llama
ávida,
a mirarla,
a gozarla,
a violarla,
o a enjugarla.

La linfa,
la tinta,
la carne,
la sangre
o el agua,
me urgen
en su albura mágica.

La página blanca,
abierta y estática,
tienta a un mismo tiempo
mi cuerpo
y mi alma.

from *Poemas* (1975)

POEM AT MIDNIGHT

The virgin page offers its naked self
in skin and tears,
on my desk,
on a clear night.

Its tender clarity calls
keenly desirous,
for me to look at it,
to enjoy relations with it,
to violate it,
or to console it.

The lymph,
the ink,
the meat,
the blood,
the water
entice me
with the magic of perfect whiteness.

The white page,
open and ecstatic,
touching at once
my body
and my soul.

CANCION POR MIS VEINTE AMORES DESESPERADOS

Mi primer amor fue Mercedes, una negra martiniqueña que tenía los brazos lustrosos y pronunciaba las erres como jotas. Fue también mi primera niñera. Yo tenía cuatro años. Mi segundo amor fue una cocinera mexicana llamada Lorenza. Tenía un rostro de ídolo indígena y una larga trenza negrísima. Se casó y murió de parto. Me enseñó a tomar café.

Mi tercer amor fue una habanera bellísima. Tenía dieciocho años. Se llamaba Marta y había sido Miss Piscina en un club social aristocrático. Siempre la recuerdo cuando escucho la canción: "Marta, capullito de rosa". La letra es muy cursi pero me eternece el recuerdo.

Mi cuarto amor fue una compañera del colegio de monjas donde aprendí a leer. Era rubia, sonrosada y grande. Se llamaba Isabel. Nunca me miró siquiera, pero las miradas que yo le dedicaba fueron interpretadas como dirigidas a ella por Raquel, una muchacha atlética y trigueña de ojos verdes, a quien conquisté ingenuamente.

Mi sexto amor fue una robusta muchacha llamada Iris, cuyo padre tenía un apellido italiano muy cacofónico. Nunca le simpaticé. Aún recuerdo sus piernas y su caballera suelta.

Mi séptimo amor fue mi profesora de francés. Ella podía ser mi abuela, pero su cuerpo grácil y sus canas me fascinaban. Había sido amiga de la Infanta Eulalia y esto le confería cierto majestuoso atractivo.

Mi octavo amor fue Guadalupe. Por supuesto era mexicana. Tenía las manos más bellas que he visto pero me doblaba en estatura. Su perrito me mordió y tuve que ponerme la vacuna antirrábica.

Mi noveno amor fue una dama francesa de exquisita educación. Ella me enseñó mucho de lo poco que sé para desenvolverme socialmente. Murió cerca de mí. Recuerdo vivamente el perfume que usaba: "Nuit de Noel", de Caron. Mi décimo amor fue la sobrina de la dama mencionada. Me decepcionó cuando me obsequió con un pastel de manzana, que me provocó un quebranto intestinal severo.

Mi onceno amor fue Sonia, una princesa rusa que menciona Malaparte en su famosa novela *La Piel.* El problema fue que la conocí cuando ella acababa de arribar a los ochenta años y sólo le quedaba un diente.

Mi décimo segundo amor fue Beatriz, una muchacha menuda y ambiciosa que quería realizarse y me impulsó a realizarme. Como estoy realizado se lo agradezco. Le debo mis buenas notas en el bachillerato. Mi décimo-tercer amor fue Alicia. Tenía los dientes afilados y los ojos claros. Su peligrosidad nos separó. Sobre ella escribí un poema.

Mi décimo-cuarto amor fue María Mercedes. Era dos años mayor que yo. Seria, sensual, y leal a un tiempo. En gran parte debo agradecerle mi éxito en los estudios universitarios. Mi décimo-quinto amor fue Evita. Ella siempre pensó que me había conocido hacía miles de años. Actualmente tiene cuatro hijos y un nieto. Mi décimo-sexto amor fue Ana. Tenía muy poca salud y un corazón cargado de sueños y pasiones puras.

Mi décimo-séptimo amor fue Alice, una venus de Maillol de carne y hueso, sobre todo de carne. Mi décimo-octavo amor fue Bebita, una estatua de Onix, tallada por Cellini . . . pero con ideas marxistas.

Mi décimo-noveno amor fue María, madrileña, de rancio abolengo. Hubiera tenido valor para posar para Goya, pero le faltó valor para saltar conmigo a América. Mi vigésimo amor, por supuesto, fue mi esposa . . .

25 de noviembre de 1985

SONG FOR MY TWENTY LOVES OF DESPERATION

My first love was Mercedes, a black woman from Martinique who had lustrous arms and pronounced her R's like J's. She was also my first nanny. I was four years old. My second love was a Mexican cook named Lorenza. She had the face of an Indian idol and a long braid that was as black as it could be. She got married and died in giving birth. She taught me to drink coffee.

My third love was a beautiful woman from Havana. She was eighteen. Her name was Marta and she had been Miss Swimming Pool at an aristocratic social club. Always I remember her when I hear the song, "Marta, My Little Rosebud." The song is tacky but makes the memory tender for me.

My fourth love was a companion at the school taught by nuns where I learned to read. She was a blond, pink as a blush, and big. Her name was Isabel. She would never even look at me, but the looks I dedicated to her were taken by Raquel as directed at Raquel herself, an athletic girl and olive-skinned and green-eyed, whom I conquered ingenuously.

My sixth love was a robust girl named Iris, whose father had a cacophonous Italian name. She never gave me a tender thought. Even now I remember her legs and free-flowing head of hair.

My seventh love was my French teacher. She could have been my grandmother, but her slender body and gray hairs fascinated me. She had been a friend of Princess Eulalia and this conferred on her a certain attractive majesty.

My eighth love was Guadalupe. Of course she was a Mexican. She had the most beautiful hands I have seen but she was twice my size. Her little dog bit me and I had to have shots for rabies.

My ninth love was a French woman of excellent education. She taught me much of the little that I know about revealing myself socially. She died nearby. I vividly remember her perfume: "Nuit de Noel," by Caron. My tenth love was the niece of the lady just mentioned. She tricked me when she gave me some apple pie that made me severely sick to my stomach.

My eleventh love was Sonia, a Russian princess that Malaparte mentions in his famous novel *The Skin*. The problem was that I knew her when she had already passed eighty years of age and she only had one tooth.

My twelfth love was Beatrice, a tiny and ambitious girl who wanted to find fulfillment and spurred me to fulfill myself. As I am fulfilled, I am thankful to her. I owe her my good grades in high school. My thirteenth love was Alicia. She had sharp teeth and clear eyes. Her dangerousness drove us apart. About her I wrote a poem.

My fourteenth love was Maria Mercedes. She was two years older than I. At once serious, sensual, and loyal. In large measure I must thank her for my success in my university studies. My fifteenth love was Evita. She always thought that she had known me for thousands of years. Now she has four children and a grandchild. My sixteenth love was Ana. She was in poor health and her heart was filled with pure dreams and passions.

My seventeenth love was Alice, a Venus de Maillol of flesh and blood, above all flesh. My eighteenth love was Bebita, an onyx statue, crafted by Cellini . . . but with Marxist ideas.

My nineteenth love was Maria, from Madrid, of long-established heritage. She had the nerve to pose for Goya, but she lacked the nerve to jump with me to America. My twentieth love, of course, was my wife . . .

THREE - *Poems*

NEIGHBORLY SUSPICION

no fence
but we kept the line

nothing to say
but being neighbors we talked

not far from death she was glad
that I was now her neighbor

the ones before were terrors
spilling out of doors

talking foul in high voices
peeing on the lawn

she was afraid she said
to call the sheriff

a week later she thought
what might they do in revenge

what scared her most was when
at three in the afternoon

they drew the curtains
every shade and all the curtains

what did they do inside
what shame did they hide

that could not face
the day

she's dead now
her darkness has fallen

now I try to close out the night
window by window

like a mantle on my shoulders
I feel her neighborly suspicion

CROW

for Frank Gollonik

a crow
blacker than black
its song
aw   you know   aw
its song   song
black   black

just a crow
not the raven of Poe
eating my neighbor's corn
even though

he puts a can
on every ear
crow gets it off
crow gets corn anyway
a crow

a crow among other crows
some lesser   some greater crows
a practical   methodical   orderly crow
grasping with learned crow feet the erudite branch
cupping with pensive crow wings the philosophical air
warming at ethereal chimneytops the deep crow soul
talking high crow talk
talk   talk

a crow
blacker than black
its song
aw   you know   aw
its song   song
black   black
talk   talk

THE RIGHT TO BEAR ARMS

When I went to the warehouse to buy dynamite,
the clerk pushed forms across the counter:
the white is for identification,
the pink is for purpose,
the blue is for insurance,
and the green is for permission.
You pay your fees,
have each one stamped;
then dynamite can be sold.

When I went to Chrysler Corporation to buy a tank,
the foreman said the tanks were not for sale.
This is military production, he said,
and these units are sold only to the army
or to a foreign government.

When I went to the Pentagon to buy the bomb,
a general said the bomb was secret.
He said there are stories in magazines
about how to make it,
and I might be able to make a connection
from Pakistan to Italy through Libya
but U.S. bombs are U.S. bombs.
Can you imagine, he asked, what might happen
if one of these got in the wrong hands?

So I went to a hock shop and bought a pistol.
I went to the warehouse, shot the clerk,
and took a box of dynamite.
I took the dynamite to Chrysler,
blew the doors off the plant,
and drove away in a tank.
I drove to the Pentagon,
shelled the office of the general
and towed away the bomb.

Now I am at home:
there have been no complaints all night.

MY FATHER HEARD A STORY

My father heard a story from his father.
A hunter pursued a beast and had it trapped,
but the beast became a tree.
The hunter got his priest and they returned.

They cut the tree, carved an idol, built a house for it,
and put the idol in the house.
But the idol ran away. The hunter pursued,
found the idol in the forest and bagged it to bring it home.

When the hunter arrived, the bag was empty.
My father told me this story. He heard it from his father.
Being a son, I did not accept my father's word
and I, too, pursued my beast among the trees.

I set out with my knife and bag, defiantly sure.
I saw the beast and had him trapped, but the beast became
a hundred trees, a hundred feet tall,
calm and proud as the wind.

Now no priest will return with me to the forest.
There is no idol in my home.
There is only my father's story, told to him by his father,
and now the story mocks me.

RUNNING JOKE

even now, it chases me

like a husband
chasing the lover
of his naked wife

and that music—
that tittering music,
that jittering, frantic calliope, flute, and drums
that accelerating parade of cats, dogs, motorcycles,
horses, horns, walls, whips, doorways, and trees

Death itself for the millionth time
singing a comic lament
slow dancing in a dirge of laughter

lighting a cigarette
putting it out
lighting it again

telling for the ten millionth time
bad breath
carious teeth
that corny, thorny, jolting joke

we all know
and never interrupt

THE ART OF GOING AWAY

When she left her home town,
when she left the ones who had watched her grow,
when she said goodbye to Mom and Dad,
who stood waving, smiling in the yard,
when she pulled down the lever
that put her in reverse,
she had not told lies
to explain lies she had told
and she was remembered as a babe
poking at a flower, playing with an ant.

When she left college,
when she shook hands with deans and honored guests,
when she delivered her valedictory address
on the need for permanent peace,
she had not yet scorned
the boredom of marriage,
and the audience applauded and approved.

When she left her first job,
where she knew her customers' names,
where she learned her business sense
and earned her boss's trust,
she had not had her first affair
and in the note her employer wrote
he said she was loyal,
a real hard worker,
a woman sure of herself
and surely moving up.

When she left her husband and three children,
the twins Tammy and Tanya,
and two-year-old Todd,
when she parked the wood-trim stationwagon
and walked away from Super-Valu,
she did not blame her in-laws,
her husband, or the church,
and her priest explained
that she was on the brink—
she somehow needed more.

On the day she sold the van she drove
from Boston to Big Sur,
on the day she decided
that vegetables alone are not enough,
on the day she determined
that mantras move no mountains,
on the day she boxed her books
and left the commune in a Ford from Hertz,
she had not betrayed her Rolls-Royce guru,
she had not wept on Oprah's shoulder
that she had been abused
by her parents   her boss   her husband   her priest   her yogi,
and happy as she left at night,
dancers robed in blue and white
strew petals in her path.

When she abandoned her polished desk
in a skyline tower,
when she kissed technology goodbye
and bid farewell
to the talking, blinking, winking world
of number crunch and doing lunch,
she had not been indicted,
and had not served a sentence,
and Diane Sawyer saw her
as a substantive success.

When she had a breast removed
and then another,
when doctors took
her ovaries and uterus,
when chemo left her bald and wasted,
when her last breath
rose and fell in her chest,
when she was lowered into the earth,
when the last dirt was tamped upon her grave,
she had not shaken her fist at Heaven
and every executive
and all of her associates
and each acquaintance

paused in passing to remember
her art in going away.

TRUTH

I have seen Truth with a video camera mounted on its tip
I have seen the grainy softness
       of back-and-white negativity
       showing Truth in flight
       closing in on its target
       going "right in the front door"
       or slipping "right down the chimney"
and I have seen the instant before the explosion of Truth
and the snowy image when Truth was gone.

I have seen the Brownian motion of Truth
        the frantic undulation and multiplication of Truth
        like an eager virus seizing a host.
I have seen Truth on the body like lesions
the lungs of Truth filled with fluid
Truth in a hospital bed
with a vacant stare.

I have seen Truth in helmets and bulletproof vests
        behind bulletproof shields.
        I have seen Truth climbing ladders
        and going in windows
        Truth ramming down walls
        Truth backing off to watch the flames.

I have seen the ethnic cleansing of Truth
        the ultimate racial purity and sexual preference of Truth
        Truth in systematic and relentless rape
        Truth in not enough of anything.

I have seen the nominee Truth
the candidate Truth
in suit and tie
Truth on Sunday-morning talk-news-show
diligent   serious   faithful   Truth
like a tightly wound reel
fresh as a reporter's smile.

I have seen Space Shuttle Truth
on its launch pad of verity
juiced with rocket language
its rainbow crew sunk into foamy sockets
its boosters stacked like facts.

I have seen experiments in space
       the astronaut who tests the Bible
       in the weightless environment
       and lets words float free from the page
       to drift and rearrange.
              She takes off her spacesuit
              turns like Salome in a dance for Herod
              veiled among the floating words of God . . .

I have seen the moon Truth
       revolving in its sky of lies
       the half moon   the quarter moon
       the sly crescent moon
       the gray   balding   dome

           Truth shining like a plate.

BLOWN BUT NOT

Blown but not
like road rubber ripping
not like
not at all like
round rolling blowing

Blown like
whale spout blowing

Blown but not
like loose leaf lost
not like
not at all
like lined legal
paper from a pad

Blown like a horn
polished and hot

Blown but not
like brain breath blowing
not like
not at all like
being being blown

Blown like glass
prismatic and clear

BROTHER, OUR MOTHER

Brother,
Our mother
Of the night
Is the river.

Not the craggy moon,
Whose craters bear no life,
Whose light is not
of its own making.

Not the tinny stars
Of constellations,
Whose light is faint
Or stopped beyond the clouds.

Brother,
Our mother
Of the night
Is the river.

Find the river mother,
Her silent banks,
Her first falls,
The ice in the hills of her source.

DO I KNOW YOU?

Do I know you seven days
Or do I know you seven years?

If I know you seven days
And speak in wavering voice
And kiss you
Then I do not know you.

>   You should not confide.
>   You must not trust.
>   There is no meaning
>   In my eyes.

But if I know you seven years
And speak to you in even tones
And take your hand, marking lines of faith,
Then I know you well.

>   You should unfold your life.
>   You must believe I will accept.
>   There is friendship
>   In my eyes.

EVERYTHING

On this island
is the cave of the sun and the moon.

Here is the mansion of the dead.
Here my soul lies in light with all souls.

Tonight, the soul of a woman
once gone into the night
comes back to this world
and finds warmth.
She is beautiful:
the sum of kindness.

Everything for me is here.

WHERE THE CITY MEETS THE WOOD

I am in the wood,
frost upon the pane,
leaves gone from October trees,
a dream of you in my mind
like snowflakes fixed upon my eyes.

You are in the city,
soot upon the window,
your building brown like a brick tree,
a poem in your hand
like a candle on a plate.

In the poem
a woman ascends a stairway.

Foot to step, foot to step,
her hand soft upon the balustrade,

she climbs to that place
where traffic blooms like wild flowers,

where subways glide like swans on lakes,
where the skyline waves with wheat.

She climbs to that place made possible in the poem,
where the city meets the wood.

MURAL OF MY WORLD

Pasted to the wall, my world meets my eyes,

the curve of the land suspended,

seas impossibly calm.

Why as my eyes meet the world

do I see *you* in the Y of the world

wearing those rubber clothes I can never imagine,

you amazing on the parallel bars of latitude,

you on a bike crossing the Atlantic,

you swimming in the sky above Arabia?

Why now *you*, like Morocco,

rising through Gibraltar, Cartagena,

your eyes, my world, your eyes,

looking back from Barcelona,

charting, mapping,

encompassing my world?

My world, my love, is you.

A QUESTION FOR HIGH PHYSICS

There is a custom among street people that a territorial claim may be made to a special spot.

A particular person who on a daily basis comes to a particular place can say that the place is his. He can say that place is his spot.

For example, in Manhattan, just south of 112th Street, on the east side of Broadway, there is a storefront, and in front of the store a drainage duct comes out of the sidewalk. It's brass and it extends about fifteen inches up from the sidewalk and it curls over like the handle of a cane. The top is flat and a person can sit on it.

A particular man sits on this duct every day and he has made it his spot. From this spot he observes those who pass on Broadway, and inasmuch as he has a claim to the territory, he exerts his right to comment.

He goes well beyond appeals for change or food, which to him are trivial. He is candidly astute in his insights about fashion and science. Gifted with the perspective and penetrating eyes of an underground man, he sees right on through to elemental truth, and he unabashedly announces his truth to the world on Broadway. He sees mothers with their children, executives with their briefcases, students with their haircuts, couples in their walk. He is detached, yet he sees how others fit in and knows he could never fit in. He seeks no solace, for he knows his place in life—his spot. He addresses people who pretend not to hear him and callously quicken their step to be at a distance from him—but they hear him, and he knows it.

When my wife and I had an apartment around the corner from this man's spot, we noticed him on various occasions. I passed him on the way to the West Side Market for fruit and bread. My wife passed him on her way to the train. He said nothing to us or about us.

I must advise you that on appearances my wife and I are conspicuously different. I am six foot four, about two seventy-five. My hair is reddish blond, and my skin is so fair that you can see the veins in the underside of my forearms. Though I speak Spanish, my first language is English. My wife, on the other hand, is short—just over five feet tall. She is from the Caribbean, and though she knows English well, she is more comfortable in Spanish. And she is black.

On a threatening afternoon—that is to say an afternoon that gave the appearance that it might rain—my wife and I came around the corner. Because the sky was dark, my wife had an umbrella in her hands. We were headed downtown to a show or museum or program. On Sunday afternoons in New York we were always headed somewhere, and we walked down Broadway to get the train.

The underground man saw us and rose immediately from his spot. He advanced toward us, gesticulating confidently, seizing his stage. With his finger in the air, he might as well have been Richard Burton.

"The question is," he said, with his eyes enlarging for emphasis, "The question is Who's going to hold the umbrella?"

He turned to go back to his spot, completely satisfied with his pronouncement, but he kept looking at us over his shoulder, still waving his finger.

"That's a question for *high* physics," he added, and he sat down on his duct. "High physics," he repeated, looking down, with professorial resolve.

We descended the stairs to the platform of the train, not fully aware of the high sentence of the underground man. But now, with years gone by, we savor what he said. We now anticipate reactions from those who might question or reject us, overtly or covertly, whether from white or black or other worlds, and we laugh.

"Who's going to hold the umbrella?" we say to each other, and we laugh.

ALL RIGHT   OK   ALL RIGHT

for Melvin Bloom

all right   OK   all right
I'll sell my car
1968 Chevy II
first car I ever had
still have
but I'll sell it
it's all rusted out
doesn't really run good
in the winter
Judge Souter took one look and drove away
in a tan 74 Dodge all nicked up
loose and dangling bumper
didn't even drive the Nova

> that's no va
> says Angel
> the boy next door
> you know, no va, ha, ha

all right   OK   all right
all right   OK   all right
I'll sell this house
across the street from where I work
I'll move to the house
with the skylights and vinyl siding
with the jacuzzi whirlpool
overlooking the lake
I'll move into a maintenance-free world
with central air
central vac
chandeliers and tile floors
I'll sell this house
I bought and fixed up
with my father
argued with him all the time
didn't do anything right
yelled at each other
never let up
got it fixed up
I'll sell it
OK   all right   OK
OK   all right   OK

all right, I'll shave my beard
I'll shave my head
I'll shave the hair around my cock
all right   OK   all right   OK   all right
I'll get a new suit
lose some weight
stop drinking
stop watching baseball
stop reading Jack Kerouac   Allen Ginsberg   Edgar Allan Poe
Christopher Columbus   Geoffrey Chaucer
Geoffrey of Monmouth   Julius Caesar   Shakespeare
Jesus Christ

I'll wear a new and narrow tie
all right   OK   all right
I'll write the book I'm supposed to write
no cars or fathers or beards
no houses   no doors   no windows
nothing but dignified   informed   flowing   prose

all right, I'll sell my sandals
my pants   the shit in my shorts
they can have it
all right   OK   all right
they can have it
name the price
and I will stand in the rain
until men come out of dark buildings
until birds fill the trees
until fish draw down the nets
until I go out walking in the 1950's
until all right becomes OK   OK becomes all right

all right   OK   all right
all right   OK   all right

WHEN THE LAST OF MY SKIN HAS ENTERED

Last night
it was something I said
or should have said
or should have heard you say
you couldn't be near me
much less embrace
or kiss   last night

but this morning
in this unheated
northwoods September house
on tile
you are barefoot
shivering

this morning
I lift the down
and down you come
all things
said unsaid unheard
in wordless warmth
forgotten

SHE TELLS ME HER DREAM
AS WE WALK ALONG THE BEACH

We came to a river
and you wanted to go ahead across
but I wasn't sure if we should go.

You were wearing those brown pants,
you know, the new ones, that go well
with your shoes and shirt.

We were in Florida, and it doesn't make sense,
but you crossed the river—very clear water.

You got your shoes all wet
and the bottom part of your pants.

I saw the big wall—the dam.
I stayed on this side.

I had to pass the high, tall wall
and I thought I would lose my balance.

I had seeds for Caribbean flowers
but you said that in Wisconsin if they grew, they'd freeze.

This was in English, not Spanish.
You said it would be all right.

SMOKE

My mind is like smoke rising
from a burning enemy camp.
Sweetness in the smoke
quickens breath and pulse.

Anacaona dances.
Her voice spirals like smoke
as she turns like the sea or the sun.

I rise like smoke and stand,
arms akimbo, in my forest.

I stand as if the last European is gone,
as if the trees and mountains and moon and waves
again are mine
like smoke.

FLIGHT

this jet rises
over clouds
its wing pricking stars
from the chest of the sun

my eyes clog with smiles
so behind my eyes
I hijack myself
parachute out of myself
back into my childhood

where I run
my arms outstretched
eyes tightly closed
jet-engine sounds
my feet off the ground

getting where this plane
will never go

MR. MUSE IS ON HIS WAY

In a silver tower Mr. Muse is getting ready,
probably shaving or grooming his hair.
He fusses over everything:
his collar, his belt, his crease.

For years he has meant to show his face
and do his part for me
but for all the times that Mr. Muse
has had his ticket,
been on his way,
arriving Tuesday at two o'clock,

not once have I heard his steps on my stoop,
not once has he entered my house,
not once has he sat at my table.

In a week I get a note:
a typist writes that Mr. Muse is sorry
but Mr. Muse had a conflict
and could not visit me Tuesday.
Is next Thursday at four all right?

The phone rings and it is Mr. Muse:
Thursday at four is now impossible
But we must see each other soon, really.

In 1996 you expect a man like Muse to miss a stitch
but isn't everything important?
Mr. Muse, how do you judge?

At this minute I know Mr. Muse is on his way.
With attaché in hand he descends his tower
in a private elevator.
He crosses a luxurious lobby,
exits through a huge brass door,
and steps royally to the curb.

Mr. Muse, I shout, I am at your service,
but he hails a shining cab
and I see the city take him . . .

GOD'S WHEELS

God has Himself some wheels
classy   convertible sporty   loaded
with leather interior
top-of-the-line CD
adjustable steering wheel
pearl-handle shifter
and power seat.

He goes around through galaxies
chirping tires   leaving rubber
with all the moons and planets watching
   sighing   oohing   ahing
and He feels *so* good, dear God.

And who can blame Him
what with all the shit He takes from Man
and Woman
what with all the doing unto others
before they can do unto others
what others have done unto them.

God deserves His car
and when He gets to the cosmic straightaway
when the universe is stripped and wide
when time and space flap at His throat
like a wind-blown stellar scarf
He deserves to see what that baby can do.
He deserves to make eons eat His dust.
He deserves to really blow the Real
right out His limitless pipes.

Dear God, He deserves to feel so good.

GOD'S SEAT

I find my mother praying,
not kneeling,
not stooped by her bed,
but sitting in the front room
in a stiff chair
with eyes closed
and light in the room.

She prays without rosary,
no candles lit,
no Bible or book of prayer
in the clasp of her hands.
In this room
on this afternoon
my mother says her prayers.

Her prayers go up, I am sure.
They go up through curtains
smooth and sheer and perfectly pinned.
They go up through light and sky,
past gates brightly calm.

There, upon another simple seat,
her silent God is listening.

JESUS WITH A BIG RADIO

Then Jesus came across the Sheep Meadow,
Bearing a big radio.
With knobs and chrome His transistor shined,
And bracing it on His shoulder
Jesus took the music,
And set His vital smile.

(It was Easter and it was eighty
In Central Park, the warmest Easter
In my memory. The parade of bonnets
And patent leather had vanished,
And the park was flashing with faces:
        vendors with carts, some with umbrellas;
        children in the zoo, some with balloons;
        friends on blankets on the grass,
        some with fruit and wine.)

The sound from His radio was visible,
Like the undulation of rising heat.

Like cars in traffic the tones were many.
The rhythms changed before I knew them.

I watched Him walking on His way
And nearly knew His grief.
I heard His music drop and fade
And tried to sense its truth.
When He was gone I moved to follow
And almost found His path.

A CRACK TO CRAWL INTO

After the failure of politics, ecology, sociology,
    literature, human faith, and personal interaction,

After nuclear confrontation, devastation, destruction,
    radiation, slow death, chaos, and the yellow fog of
    doom,

                            two cockroaches meet
                            in what was once Wyoming.

Survivors of the blast, impervious to its effects, these
    roaches touch feelers and remember.

They remember the day a uniformed exterminator forced them
    deep into a crack in the damp basement wall of
    Mrs. Hildegard Jennings, who always feared roaches
    more than she feared or even thought about the nuclear
    termination of human civilization.

The roaches remember the painful, penetrating vapors of the
    past—the sticky, noxious fluids and resins.

The roaches remember the eyes of those who hated bugs, those
    who smashed roaches with rolled newspapers, those who
    crushed brown beetles under hateful shoes, those who
    screamed in horror at the sight of many-legged, rapidly
    running creatures

                            among plates and pots
                            left standing in a sink.

"They got themselves," says the first roach, surveying the
    stillness all around her, her antennae flexing in
    delight.

"Yes," says the second roach, his senses alive with the sex
    of a million generations. "They had no crack to crawl
    into."

GRAY

He knew he was old
when he heard Mantovani
on the car radio and liked it—

when he heard 101 Strings
play *Michelle*

when he heard Enoch Light
play *The Way We Were*

he began to think that it was OK
and he liked it.

But he didn't know what to say
thought he had gone completely gray

when he heard Easy Listening Light FM
the Relaxing Sound of Beautiful Music

spin a soft, muted medley of Megadeth
play a Zamfir pan-flute arrangement of Guns n' Roses
play an elevator-music, music-to-drill-teeth-by,
supermarket P.A. version of Eazy E:

"Ah," he said, feeling very gray,
"Fuck the Police."

MY DISAPPOINTMENT ABOUT A CONTEMPTUOUS PERSON, WHOSE CONTEMPT WAS ONCE ADMIRABLE, BUT NOW IS WORTHLESS

I wish that we could go back to the way it was before.

I wish we could go back to when you did not acknowledge my existence and did not let your eyes meet mine and did not exchange words or respond to my greeting or accept anything that I did or anything I said as anything, as anything at all.

I wish we could go back to you ignoring me, the good feeling.

I want to go back and bask in the completeness of your exquisite rejection of me without consideration or examination or thought for any part of my personality or individuality. I want to go back to the time when I savored your absolute dismissal of any possibility of communication or recognition or exchange or friendship. There were purity and dignity in your invention of my invisibility, pleasure in your provocation of the quiet pangs of my need to know you and have your confidence, so much purity and dignity in your refusal ever to allow any of that to happen in even the slightest degree, in even the shadow of the slightest degree.

I wish we could be like that again.

I wish we could go back to the way it was when I was sure of who you were and yet puzzled over who you really were and tried to figure out what I could say to you to show to you that I knew who you were and what you were about, that I was not like the others who were part of all the others who gathered all the others around them with all the others. I wish we could go back to when you were steadfast and proud and aloof and infinitely within yourself, when you had the divine coldness of someone sharpening a knife in a dim kitchen, someone talking to himself and sharpening a knife.

But now you have surrendered all.

Now you have in less than a second of unintended acknowledgment, in less than an inadvertent glance, in less than a blink of momentary recognition (even if at once withdrawn), revealed your once impenetrable privacy. Now you have downloaded to me the inside of your head, and I sit at the desk behind your eyes. I pull out all the drawers, read all your papers, toss them to the floor.

In a flickering of eternity in your eyes I see your family and feel the way your grandmother felt as she felt faulty sidewalk under her feet, feel the way your father felt when he drove his new car over an old bridge, feel the way your wife felt when for the first time you were serious and sincere, feel the way your baby felt when you took him in your arms.

Oh, dear friend, how I hate you now!

I hate you because, even if not by intention, you wavered and gave up the wall, the fence, the glass, the hedge, the shield, the barrier, the mountain, the river, the door, the impassable border.

I hate you because now I know you as I know myself.

HOMAGE TO MINOSO

Ay, Minoso!

black Cuban in the American League
1949
because the field is the universe
and as fielders we are fellows
you raised your calloused hands
picked up a bat in the American League

Ay, Minoso!

White Sox and Indians
White Sox and Indians
the Cards
Minnie! Your baseball card—

your line-drawn face   your eyes like orbs
you a wise man banging out hits for Jesus!
        your name—same as the name
        of a wrinkled gray-haired aunt—
Minnie!

And who is it, Minoso, who stops you now,
now seventy times around the base paths of the sun?
Who are these clowns, these Sox?

Didn't Nolan Ryan punch any sense into Robin Ventura?
        For whom is Frank Thomas the Big Hurt?
        What vice, Ron Karkovice?
        Was it you, Ozzie Guillen?
        What do you know, BO?

Take your losses, Sad Sox!
Go on thinking you'll never grow old!
Go hitless, Sad Sox,
Go down, down, down
to ignominious defeat (yeah, you know so!)

until you wish
Minnie would swing his bat
line a homer
the crowd standing

to see the ball's flight
the crowd standing
for Minoso rounding the bases
dirt flying from epic cleats
Minoso!
tipping his cap
to seven decades

THE DEATH OF BOB DYLAN

The guilty undertaker sighs
and the lonesome organ grinder cries.
Bob Dylan is dead.

It's all over now for Baby Blue.
He ain't gonna work on Maggie's farm
no more.

His vision in the final end
has shattered like the glass.
He's seen his light go shining
into the dream that has no number.

He won't get one more cup of coffee before he goes.
Highway 61 is closed.
Oh, Mama, you took that badge off him:
he was so tangled up in blue,
he was knockin' on heaven's door,
he was on Desolation Row.
Mama! This really is the end—
he's nailed inside his coffin
with the Memphis Blues again.

But who among you could tell
just who fell
and who was left behind?

Who among you do you think could bury him,
so alone and terrified,
with his sad-eyed lady of the lowlands
and the sad-eyed prophet who says
that no man comes?

No martyr is among you now
whom you can call your own.
Dylan is set down in his grave
and you stone him.

Oh, you say, he's got everything he needs,
he's an artist, he don't look back.

You say he's out riding on his chrome horse
with his diplomat
who carries on his shoulder
a Siamese cat.

You say nobody has to guess
that Dylan can't be blessed
because you've seen finally
that he's like all the rest.

You say the rooster crows at the break of dawn.
You look out your window and Dylan is gone.
You don't think twice—
it's all right.

You say there's something going on
and you know exactly what it is—
Dylan, Mr. Jones.

I have a lot of nerve
to say I am his fan.

I'm looking for someone
who's never weak but always strong
someone who will die for me and more.

I dream I am amongst the ones
who put him out to rest.

Dylan is so much older now
he was younger than this once.

I really have a lot of nerve
to say I am his fan.

Now that he's gone,
I just stand here grinning.

WITHOUT SUCCESS, THE NATIONALLY ACCLAIMED POET DISGUISES HIS ALCOHOLISM

The secretary for the distinguished, difficult-to-reach agent
representing the urbane, widely anthologized, nationally acclaimed poet
tells Ophelia Willow that the poet can possibly come to campus in May,
for ten thousand dollars, and expenses.

In May, at the airport, the poet descends from the heavens.
In flight, he has spit up on his tie
and though he has laundered himself
in the lavatory on the plane,
when he enters our car, the odor is all.

Ophelia and I pretend not to notice.

In town, at the Quality Inn, the poet dismisses us,
says he needs to rest, wants to review for the reading.
Will we pick him up at seven?
We leave, and he wanders toward the motel lounge.

At seven he is drunk,
strangely, deeply, fully drunk,
drunker than all the whiskey he has wolfed,
but steady, stable, and menacingly ready to read.

Dr. Icarus introduces the poet to a spellbound audience,
extolling the poet's achievement,
commending his sensitivity.
The reading begins.

The nationally acclaimed poet recites
from his celebrated series of sonnets,
his sequence of surreal sestinas.
He leaves the podium, descends the stairs of the stage,
and stands among his listeners.
Slow and sonorous, he is resonant with sense and sentiment.
He intoxicates the hall.

Later, in the Crosby Room,
where champagne sparkles in crystal,
where chandeliers glow over women in impossible shoes,
where men wave cigarettes to emphasize their cloudy thoughts,
the poet, quite frankly, is rude.

He is rude, especially, to Ophelia Willow,
whom he berates for ignorance of the classics,
for shallow, self-serving, indulgent confessions.
He is rude to her in front of all her students and fellow faculty.
Ophelia rushes tearfully from the room,
with allies in lace pursuing.

Unsteady, the poet himself then leaves.
I find him in the lavatory, kneeling at a stool,
in what now, I suppose, is the normal cycle of his nausea.
I help him to his feet, and he puts full trust in my kindness.
I drive him to the motel and set him in his bed.

At dawn, I take him to the airport.
He says he sees me as a genuine writer,
smiling as he shares the subtlety of Homer
and the satirical sweetness of Eliot.
When he is sure that my eyes are fixed upon the road,
he tips a flask he pulls from his jacket.

At the terminal, he says he'll just get out, grab his bag.
I shake his hand and wish him well—

He ascends the ramp to where doors automatically part,
then heads for the airport bar.

SWIMMING FOR BERRIES

I am smiling
because I am thinking
of bears
swimming for berries.

Superior is cold
even in summer a killer
but from island to island
bears swim for berries.

I am smiling
because I see myself
big as a bear
among the bears

they in their fur
I in my skin
in the chill of the lake
swimming.

Water like ice
but bears don't mind!
Swim swim swim
swim swim swim swim

So sweet
these thoughts of bears
this taste of berries
full and sweet   full and sweet
so sweet   so sweet
so sweet!

FOOD FEELINGS

As a citizen
interested in fairness
and consideration
for all
especially animals
and plants
I cook and eat
I object
to insensitive barbarous indecent
still-don't-get-it
language.

Last night
for example
in a moment of reflection
chomping on celery
I realized that it
(poor pale green thing!)
must be hurt
must resent
facile unfeeling connection
dumb knee-jerk association
with stalking.

And carrots
why
should they be held responsible
for prison sex?
why should bananas
melons and plums
bear the presumption
of erotic intention
perverse design?

There's all this stuff
horny bulls
strutting cocks
goosing
little piece of chicken
with
implications
the animals themselves never intended

but
nevertheless
endure
being reserved and dignified
inhabitants of earth
being cautious and nondisruptive
partners at the table.

I cannot eat in peace!
Someone should stand up
to this callous talk!
The dinner I eat
demands meaningful reform
my food refuses to be pushed around!
I want my piece of the pie
without having someone call me a fruit
a nut
a crusty old man.

Opening mouths
we must learn
think fairly
acknowledge our differences
be sensitized to food
because
I love this country
and I love to eat.

THE WAY YOU'RE GOING

better stop
cut down
get out
get yourself
get control of yourself
keep yourself
keep yourself going
you're going
soon will be gone
soon will be long gone

better stop
better cut it out
better cut it loose
get yourself
get control of yourself
keep yourself
keep yourself going
better stop
better stop and think
better think about where you've been
better think about where you're going
where you're going to be
you're going
soon will be gone
soon will be long gone

better stop
better go
better stop
better go
better stop
better go
you're going
the way you're going
to need some extra time.

I COULD NEVER WRITE A POEM

I could never write a poem about you.
Nothing about you interests my mind.
I don't have anything to say.
Your voice, hands, eyes, and shape
do not conform to a poem.
I could never write a poem about you.
Another man might write a novel
or maybe a collection of stories
about you, but I would never take the time.
There's nothing in you that makes a sentence.
And I could never write a poem about you,
not a line.

SECOND THOUGHTS ON ABANDONING THE NARRATOR OF "NOTES FROM UNDERGROUND"

Dostoyevsky's paradoxalist
cannot refrain
from going on with his notes
just as he went on about
reason and the will;
philosophy, truth, ethics, and contradiction;
the humiliation of inattention, disrespect;
pretensions to love and protect;
mad rejection of love and trust;
cold intercourse
and colder remorse.

Yet, at the end,
Fyodor and I, his reader,
we are tired of the notes
of this ridiculous man,
and we leave him.

On page 91,
Part II: A Propos of the Wet Snow,
Dostoyevsky (in italics)
goes elsewhere,
probably a warm place with a nice fire,
maybe for beer, or wine,
a place where he and I
can have fashionable
and intelligent conversation.

That is to say:
we may stop here.

WILLIAM LAWLOR (1951-   )

William Lawlor's poems, translations, short stories, critical articles, personal essays, editorial columns, and book reviews have appeared in *North Coast Review, Croton Review, South Coast Poetry Journal, Iowa Review, New Mexico Humanities Review, Negative Capability, The Milwaukee Journal-Sentinel, New York Newsday* and other journals, reviews, and newspapers. He is a recipient of a Literary Arts Fellowship and a Development Grant from the Wisconsin Arts Board. The National Endowment for the Humanities awarded him a Summer Study Grant to do research on the Beat Generation.

In Stevens Point, Wisconsin, where he is Professor of English at the University of Wisconsin—Stevens Point, he is the organizer of the Mission Coffee House Literary Arts Series, a community-based program of readings that began with an open reading on December 15, 1992. Soon support became available through Poets & Writers, the Stevens Point Arts Council, the Wisconsin Arts Board, and other sources. The series now features ten programs a year, providing a forum for local and regional writers and occasionally a nationally famous writer. Now in its fourth year, the series has included more than thirty presentations.

Lawlor's interest in translating poems written in Spanish developed slowly. Although he studied Spanish in high school and college, he sometimes claims that he learned most "from the walls of the subways of New York." He became communicative in Spanish when he lived in Santiago, the Dominican Republic, where he taught at Universidad Católica Madre y Maestra while on leave from his post in Wisconsin. He had occasion to meet baseball fans, agricultural workers, writers, painters, politicians, historians, journalists, and people in business, and this experience gave depth and range to his knowledge of Spanish. He has been translating from Spanish for fifteen years, focusing mainly on modern and contemporary writers from Latin America.

Born in Manhattan in 1951, Lawlor grew up in Queens and went to college in the Bronx, where he received his B.A. and M.A. in English from Lehman College of the City University of New York. In 1974 he moved to Indiana and taught at Ball State University, where he earned a Ph.D. in English in 1978. At the University of Wisconsin—Stevens Point, he teaches classes in creative writing, composition, and literature, including courses on eighteenth-century British literature, the Beat Generation, and the writings of James Baldwin and Gwendolyn Brooks.

QUEEN E. BROOKS

Queen E. Brooks created the cover for this book. She is a 1994 Arts Midwest Fellowship recipient who writes, "There is an African tradition of inspired vision which has permeated the African-American community since slavery. This condition continues today among the world's Black folk artists. I feel a stylistic and spiritual kinship to these skilled and visionary artists."